FROM DA BOTTOMS 2 DA TOP

MARLO DA MOTIVATOR

Copyright © 2020 Marlo Da Motivator

All rights reserved. No part of this publication may be reproduced, distributed, or transmitted in any form or by any means, including photocopying, recording, or other electronic or mechanical methods, without the prior written permission of the publisher, except in the case of brief quotations embodied in critical reviews and certain other noncommercial uses permitted by copyright law.

Book Design by Aeysha

Testimonials

"After reading Marlo's book, I would definitely recommend that anyone currently or previously incarcerated read this book. I appreciated how raw and honest Marlo was in telling his personal story growing up and going through everything he went through. It's like he's sitting right there next to you telling his story to you as you read the book. I like that he wasn't embarrassed to share strategies that he personally used to keep himself from going back to prison, regardless of what others in his neighborhood thought. I also appreciated the personal self-analysis workbooks that he provides, so someone who really feels they've hit rock bottom can make the steps to focus and climb up. I also enjoyed Marlo's use of word pictures/analogies. The one he shares about the nasty smelly old garbage meat being reused for something good and useful was motivating.

Like I always say to Marlo, you don't have to be a prison inmate to get motivated by Marlo's work, and this book is a great example of that. It's a must read!!!!"

~ **Aaron Forbes**
Self-Help Group Sponsor
Sierra Conservation Center

"It's an honest conversation!! A genuine walk with someone who knows all the rocks and holes on the path, and it is a great walk. It is a fun read and I love the work being done within it. Not just in the worksheets, but also in the questions throughout. Great work!!!

Lastly, I commend you on completing this crazy achievement. Many talk about it, few try, and even fewer commit fully as you have done. Good luck my friend!!"

~ **Dameion Renault, M.S.P**

"I love the book. Reading it is like watching your presentation to students. You write well. You don't talk down to anyone and I like the real language you use. You are positive in your approach regarding detailing your failures and success and the success that others can find if/when they make the choice to do so.

The activities are thought provoking and simple to process. This will definitely help motivate people to create a plan for success and improve their lives."

~ **Donovan Walker, M.Ed., CSCS, USAW**

From Da Bottoms 2 Da Top

"It's not where you start that defines you, you're defined by what you make of it."
~ **Marlo Da Motivator**

Instagram: https://www.instagram.com/marlodamotivator/?hl=en

Facebook: https://www.facebook.com/MarloDaMotivator

Website https://www.marlodamotivator.com/

Acknowledgments

I would like to thank God the Father, and His son Jesus Christ for not only giving me life, but for always blessing and leading me.

I want to also thank my loving, beautiful, supporting wife, who did more than just help in this endeavor, but also in every task that I take on. Thank You Sweetheart! I Love You!

To my children: thank you for being a part of the motivation that pushed me to write this book. It is my hope that as all of you read the book, you will learn more about me, and my past hurts, as well as my drive and accomplishments and our family. I also want to thank you guys for loving me even through the times that you all might not see things the way that I do. One of the things that I want for you guys in this life, is for you to win. Know always, that Daddy loves you.

To my family: I love you guys. My sisters, brothers, nieces, nephews (damn you dudes keep me working hard), cousins, aunties, uncles, and extended family, thank you for being in my life.

To Dad: I love you. I know that there are many things that I would have loved to have done with you when I was a kid. There are also many things that I wish that I did not see you do or hear you say. However, I must say that I am also overjoyed that you are still alive and that you have changed. I am excited that you and I have a great relationship and that you are my father. I love you!

Thank you to those that helped with this project, from reading my manuscript to giving me valuable feedback. You are appreciated! I will not attempt to name all of you because I may miss a name.

Lastly, I must give a big thank you to the people that told me that I couldn't win, the people that wanted to see me lose. You have been a great boost of energy for my success. Do me one favor though: Keep Hating! Your Hating is Very Motivating!

Dedication

Dedicated to the memory of my beautiful, loving, caring, talented, and God-fearing mother, Linda Ann Jackson. I love you! It took me a long time, but I finally came around to understand the things that you were trying to teach and tell me. Thank You!

11/10/1953 – 05/01/2004

"I'll Plant the Seed," was something that you always said and actually did do. I wish that you were here so that I could tell you that you were right. You did indeed plant the seed and God has grown it!
I love you momma!

Table Of Contents

Forward By Jeffrey Taylor 15

Introduction 19

Chapter 1
Dysfunctional Family 21

Chapter 2
Early Life 24

Chapter 3
The Shit No Child Should Have To Go Through! 30

Let's Talk "Learning About Ur Damn Self" 35

Chapter 4
Your Setback Was You Being Setup For Your Comeback! 39

Chapter 5
Admit Your Faults And Mistakes And Take Full Reasonability. 49

Chapter 6
Who R U And Y R U Here? 52

Chapter 7
U Got 2 Have A Fuckin' Fight Plan! 57

Chapter 8
(P.c.p) Persistence, Commitment & Perseverance 62

Let's Talk "Hard Times Makes You Bigger & Stronger" 66

Chapter 9
What Were You Called To Do? 69

Chapter 10
Get Off Of The Fucking Treadmill 74

Let's Talk "Are you ready?" 77

Chapter 11
Fuck Fear 79

Chapter 12
Open Letter 83

Let's Talk "How 2 Stay Da Fuck Out!" 86

Real Life Scenario #1 88

How I Got Out Of The Situation! 90

Real Life Scenario #2 91

A Quick Way Out 92

Chapter 13
Don't Waste Time And Don't Quit 93

Forward
By Jeffrey Taylor

I am a strong believer that some people are in our lives for only a season, while others are in our lives for years. Marlo is someone who has been in my life for multiple years. I first met Marlo when I was a Site Director for Oakland Midnight Basketball. He and a group of his friends came in as a team. They were an average team, but they were having fun. One of the prerequisites to playing in the games was attendance at the Friday night workshop. If you did not attend the workshop, you could not play. Early on in the season, Marlo and his crew missed the workshop. They showed up with a letter that they claimed their supervisor had written. Unbeknownst to them, I actually knew their boss. The funny thing about their forged letter was they spelled his name wrong. I got a good laugh, but did not allow them to play. After that episode, Marlo and his team did not miss a workshop.

The character and leadership Marlo displayed impressed me so much that I offered him a job the next summer. Although he was young, Marlo was very mature and respectful. Everyone loved him. I was so impressed with Marlo's work ethic I got him another part-time job at a video store that summer. The owner was a good friend of mine. She too was impressed with Marlo.

A few years later, I left that job and began teaching. Marlo showed up at the school to check on his nephew. I was talking to my principal about Marlo and he became impressed. He offered him a job as well. All the teachers and students loved Marlo. He is a people person. I am not sure if working at a school motivated Marlo to enroll in college, but he left after a year to go to college.

As I sat down to write this, I began to reflect on the evolution of Marlo. In doing so I realized that Marlo was really paying attention to the presentations during the Midnight Basketball workshops. Most of the workshops encompassed life skills, positive choices and goal setting. The latter of the three is where I see Marlo excelling. He completely understands that you are not done after you achieve a goal you set. Accomplishing a goal is an awesome thing; however, once you accomplish a goal, then you set another goal. I learned early on that goal setting is done in three phases: short-term (0 – 6 months); mid-term (6 months – 2 years); and long-term (2 – 5 years). This process allows you to see growth, which motivates you to keep striving for improvement. This is also how you set yourself up for constant growth. Marlo is always striving to improve himself, but what I really like about Marlo, is that he is not afraid to ask questions. Not only does he ask questions, but he applies the new knowledge to his life.

Watching how Marlo has been able to transform his life, it is befitting that he would write a book of this nature. Sometimes people offer advice based on theory. However, Marlo is not just talking the talk, but he has actually walked the walk. I love the format of the book. It allows you to reflect and take notes. If you are lost and trying to figure things out, I recommend that you read this book and complete the reflections, you will not be disappointed.

I have been blessed to have had many different jobs and meet many great people; however, I have yet to meet anyone who knows everything. You don't need to know everything, but what you do need to know is where to go get the answers to the questions you have. If you are the smartest person in your immediate circle, then you need to expand your circle. Surrounding yourself with people who are more knowledgeable than you, helps you continue to expand your knowledge base. When you lay your head down on the pillow at night, you need to reflect back on your day and ask yourself, "What did I learn today?" If you can't think of anything, then you have some changes to make for tomorrow. One of my favorite quotes comes from Albert Einstein, "Insanity is doing the same thing over and over again and expecting different results." As I previously stated, if you are not growing and becoming a better person, then you need to expand your circle and also determine if the season is over for the "friends" who are currently in your circle.

I put quotation marks around the word friend because too many of us do not really understand what it means to be a friend or even more important who deserves that title of friend from you. If you want to know if someone is your friend, call them and say you're moving and need their help or ask to borrow money and let them know you are not sure when you can pay it back. My car was repossessed once and I needed $1,700 to get it back. I didn't have a clue where I was going to get it. However, a "friend" saw that I was looking depressed and asked me what was wrong with me. When I told her, she wrote me a check for $1,700 and said, "Just pay me back when you get it, there's no rush." I couldn't believe it. She never asked me for the money back. I paid her half and several months later, I gave her the remainder plus an additional $200. She said you already paid me back, what is this for? I had to explain to her that I had only given her half and owed that to her. She remains my "FRIEND" to this day.

I consider Marlo my "FRIEND." On February 13, 2009, I was out shopping and saw Marlo. I had not seen him in a few years. We exchanged greetings and he asked me what I was doing. I explained to him that I was getting married the next day, and had to go meet my fiancé to set up for the reception. He said, I'm going to go get my wife and we're coming to help. They showed up and worked harder than some of our family members. Yes, Marlo is my "FRIEND."

Introduction

Have you ever been walking down the street, and stepped in some dog shit? You then say to yourself: Damn! Then one of the first things that come to your mind is, who in the hell has allowed their dog to shit right here, and didn't even have the fuckin decency to clean it up. The other thing that rushes into your mind is the question of how in the hell am I going to get this off of my shoe? Well growing up in Oakland, I can tell you that there were plenty of days that I felt like the dog shit in this analogy. Yea, that's right: I felt like the shit smashed underneath someone's feet. However, I found a way to wipe away that horrible feeling, sliding myself into a much better situation, as I began to take control of my life. But do not be deceived: even though you wipe dog shit off of your shoe, that doesn't mean that everything is okay. Why do you say that someone may ask? I know that because there were times that I also felt like the shoe in this analogy. I felt nothing more than mistreated, disrespected, discussed, less than, and upset. Here is the deal, once you wipe dog shit off of the bottom of your shoes, no matter how clean the shoe may look, it still has the fuckin aroma that no one wants to deal with nor around them. In the same way, even after changing the horrible situation that I was born into, as well as making the necessary changes to myself, it was obvious to me that that fucked up aroma was still there. I realized that there was still more that I needed to do, to get rid of that lingering smell. After much thought and prayer, it became clear to me that there are many other people who feel the same way that I once felt, and it was my duty to help them learn how to overcome as well. That is why I decided to write From Da Bottoms 2 Da Top.

In this book you will learn that it is not where or how you start that defines you, you are defined by what you make of it. You will learn that the mistakes that you have made, the hardships that you have experienced, the pain that you have caused and have endured are the same things that proves to you that you are a fuckin winner. It proves that you can accomplish whatever it is that you put your mind to accomplishing. I know that they have called you a "fuck up" all of your life; I know that you have been divorced several times; I know that they have told you that you do not matter, and I also know that you can't figure out a way to truly win. That's okay! Because I also know that you are a fuckin winner, and the only thing that you need to learn and hear to help you capture your confidence is right here in this book.

It was the 1994-1995, Chicago Bulls that were barely able to make it into the playoffs. They only made it in because of the return of Michael Jordan as he came out of retirement. However, the Bulls were eventually eliminated from the playoffs that year and their season was over. Nevertheless, the very next year, the 1995-1996, Chicago Bulls ripped through the next season setting a then new NBA record of wins as they won 72 out of 82 games and as they went on to capture the Championship as well. What changed? They brought in one impact person (Dennis Rodman), and that pushed them past everyone else. You have me! That's right, this book is your fuckin (Dennis Rodman). See you can be losing one minute and the fuckin Champion the next. Think about your current situation! At your current rate does it seems as if you are going to make it into the playoffs? To hell with what your current situation looks like, read this fuckin book and let's get you your championship.

Chapter 1
Dysfunctional Family

Driving down the freeway at nearly 80 miles per hour in a 1977 two-door Ford Pinto, with blood gushing from the two holes in her upper body, my mother was headed to the hospital. She had a big-ass hole in her neck and another hole in the top portion of her back. Somehow my mother was able to miraculously make it safely. I remember there were about six or seven of us crammed inside the car, yet it only sat about four people. My mother was losing blood fast, so much so she started to lose consciousness as she pulled up in front of the hospital. Before she could fully stop the car, my cousin jumped out and ran into the hospital to notify the staff that my mother needed a doctor ASAP. All of us, including my mother, rushed into the hospital where we were met by the hospital staff, and they took her straight to the emergency room. I had to be only around five or six years old, but I can remember this horrible situation as clear as day.

While she was in the emergency room laying on the gurney, a doctor approached my mother with a needle that had to be at least twelve inches long and attempted to stick it into my mother's neck. I began to scream at the doctor, "Don't stick my mother with that thing!" That scream stopped the doctor from sticking my mother with the needle, which according to the head doctor in charge saved my mother's life. How is that possible? When I screamed, that's when they realized that I was in the room and started to get me out of the room but the delay gave time for the head doctor on duty to run in and see what the other doctor was about to do with the needle. He yelled out, "No! Don't stick her with that!" I'm not sure what was inside the needle, but whatever it was would apparently have killed her.

How did we get to this situation? How did my mother end up with not one but two knife wounds in her upper body? Why is a 5 year old witnessing this type of horror? We were at one of my aunties house parties having a good time when for some reason (maybe the liquor) my auntie and mother began to exchange words. My mother told my sisters and I to go to the car because we were about to leave. While loading into the car I noticed that I had left my baseball hat inside of the house and I told my mother. She went back into the house to get my hat; her and my auntie had some more words and as my mother begun to walk down the stairs my auntie stabbed her in the top portion of her back with a large knife. According to my mother, she was able to turn around and wrestle with my auntie over the knife. The both of them fell down the stairs and as they came to the bottom of the stairs my mother had taken the knife away from my auntie but she accidently stabbed herself in the left lower portion of her neck with the knife.

My sisters and I busted through the door but not before my mother had taken the knife and stabbed my auntie in between her legs with it. We were able to break up the tussling between the two of them and make it outside of the house to the car. As we tried to get into the Pinto my auntie came to the front door with a long ass gun and pointed it at us. My mother was bleeding all over the place, I also noticed blood coming from my auntie as she pointed the long rifle at us. Thanks be to God she did not shoot as we all poured into the Pinto and my mother sped out of the driveway making her way towards the freeway.

Chapter 2
Early Life

"Instruction is good for a child; but example is worth more."
~ Alexandre Dumas

I was born in 1979 in the Fillmore district of San Francisco. I remember growing up in the 80's when weed was the big thing and people were really starting to put other drugs inside of their weed to get that extra high. As young as I was I can remember a few songs about drugs that a kid my age should not have even heard. One was called "White Horse" by Laid Back, another was "White Lines" by Grandmaster Flash, and the last one was "Girl That's Your Life" by Too Short. I can recollect seeing my older sister, cousin and their friends smoking weed so much so that, around the age of 5 or 6, me and one of my cousin attempted to emulate them.

One day we waited until everyone had left the house and we found some small weed butts inside an ashtray, we lit and smoked 7 or 8 of them. After a while we were hungry as hell and extremely tired! My sisters and a few of her friends returned home and they knew right away that we were high as a kite. I think the fact that we were complaining about being so damn hungry may have helped them realize this as well.

"Someone is always watching what you say and or do and most often it is the young person in your life."
~ Marlo Da Motivator

"It's time to stop quoting to our young people the old quote:"

"Do as I say, but don't do as I do."
~ John Selden's Table-Talk

I don't think my mother was doing drugs at this time, at least I hadn't seen her do any but I do know there was a hell of a lot of drinking going on inside of my house. My dad didn't live with us, he lived in Oakland with my step mother and my four brothers they shared together. He did come around some of the time being that he did work in San Francisco as a construction worker/carpenter not to mention that he had a lot of friends, and kicked it with hella guys from San Francisco. At some point around the age of 6, my mother must have gotten evicted because this is the first time that I can recall us living inside of a hotel and it sure wouldn't be the last. We stayed in that hotel for a while. In fact, my mom became an employee of the hotel and worked there until we moved to Oakland. It had to be around late 1985 when my mother relocated us to the other side of the bay. That's right Oakland! We moved into a small modular house on 15th and Center Street in West Oakland, a place which took on the name the Lower Bottoms or Da Bottoms for short in about 1989 or 1990.

This is when I noticed that my mother was using crack and that it was affecting not only her way of living but also it had compromised me and my sister's life style as well. Moving into Oakland was a great thing because I was closer to my dad though he didn't spend any more time with me than he did while I lived in San Francisco. On the other hand, it was a horrible thing because I think that it opened the flood gate for my mother to just get high without any refraining. Maybe she didn't hold back because she was no longer around her friends in San Francisco that didn't smoke crack, or maybe she was trying to cover up past hurt and harm. At any rate whatever the case was, she allowed the drugs to put us in situations where we had to stand in long ass lines to get that free butter, powdered milk and eggs, rice and beans and that meat in the tall ass can that was handed out in the poor communities. I believe that that tall ass silver can had a cow and a pig on the front of it. I think the best thing that they gave out was that damn block cheese. Many called it "Government Cheese". That cheese was hard to cut but it made for one hell of a cheese toast or grill cheese sandwich.

While living on 15th street, I remember my mother and father getting into a heated argument one day and my dad leaving out the door. My sisters and I were playing in the living room and at some point I jumped from one of the couches to the other and all of a sudden we heard a loud ass gun blast and I witnessed a bullet come through the living room window as glass shattered everywhere. What in the hell is going on was the question that went through my brain. I saw where the bullet hit the ceiling and made a fucking hole. Who in the fuck would shoot through a house window with kids in the living room playing? My mother came running into the living room and yelled out to us at the top of your lungs "GET DOWN". I also heard my dad voice outside cursing at my mom and then I heard my mom say. "This crazy mutha fucka is shooting at us!"

My mom slid across the floor and turned out the lights as she begun cursing at my dad telling him that he was a stupid punk mutha fucka. My dad came to the door and tried to open the door but it was locked. Still to this day, I am not sure what he was planning to do if he had gotten into the house but I am damn sure happy that we didn't find out. The next thing I know, the police had shown up within a matter of seconds. They must have been in the neighborhood already. I heard the police instruct my dad to put his hands in the air and to come down the 5 steps that lead to our back door. I ran to the window and what I saw with my own fucking eyes was some shit that one would imagine to see in a Hollywood movie or something. One of the officers approached my dad, I guess to handcuff him, while the other officer stood at a short distance away. My dad somehow grabbed the officer, spun him around placing him in some kind of choke hold. This shit looked like they were actors dressed up for a WWF match or something. While my dad was choking the shit out of the fucking cop and dragging him up the 5 steps to the back door, the other cop was screaming "Let him go!" "Let him go!"

My mom is screaming at me telling me to get away from the got damn window and door but I wasn't going to walk away from this crazy shit. The next thing I knew was the fucking cop pulled his gun out and began pointing it at my dad and his partner. He started to tell my dad that he was going to shoot his ass if he did not release his partner. At this time my dad had his back up against the back door choking the cop and kicking the door yelling out for someone to open the fucking door. My mom yelled back out to him and said, "Hell no mutha fucka!" However, I wasn't about to let them kill my dad without trying to help, so I opened the door and what I seen next was something that I still have trouble understanding to this day.

My dad released the hold that he had on the cop, pushed him towards the other cop that was aiming the gun at him. At the same time he did some sort of fucking acrobatic back roll into the house slamming the door and pushing me away from the door. The police stood outside of the house and yelled out, "Pee Wee you are a crazy mutha fucka man!" Those are the same words my mother said about my dad right before the cops arrived. I guess my mom was telling the truth about my dad being a crazy mutha fucka because the police said the same thing. Can you believe that the cops simply walked back to their car and fucking left? I don't know what happened to the gun that my dad had used to shoot through the window, but my guess is that when he saw the cops pulling up he may have had time to stash it somewhere. Now a days they would have killed his ass. Hell, we have seen in recent time's people getting killed for holding a damn cell phone or even selling loose cigarettes. My dad ass was lucky.

That wasn't the first time that I witnessed my mother and father with a gun in the mist getting violent with one another. One night my mother, my father, my uncle, and I were sitting outside in a car. I'm not sure where we were but I do know that my mother was in the driver's seat and my father was in the passenger seat. I was in the back seat behind my mother and my uncle sat behind my father. All three of them had been drinking and I would debate anyone that they were fully intoxicated. I remember my father brandishing some type of hand gun and my mother begun to yell at him. My dad feeling disrespected told my mother that he would kill her ass and as he began to lift the gun up, my mother grabbed the gun and they started tussling over it. I am sitting there wondering what in the hell is about to happen, meanwhile my uncle had a look on his face like he was looking at Satan himself. The gun accidently discharged and I remember seeing a spark of fire come from the gun and the bullet entering the dashboard. My uncle opened the rear passenger door, grabbed me out of the car and took off running with me down the fuckin street. I was crying for my mother and I could hear my parents yelling expletives at each other as my uncle made a getaway. My uncle did not stop running until we reached one of his lady friend's apartment. Once we got inside of the apartment, they put me in a room and he started to tell his friend that he thinks that my mother is dead. I couldn't believe what I was hearing. He told her, "That crazy mutha fucka Pee-Wee (which is my father's nickname), may have just killed my sister!" I am not sure when or how I got back to my parents, but I am sure like always, once the liquor wore off, everyone acted like nothing had happened.

Chapter 3
The Shit No Child Should Have To Go Through!

"You're not a victim for sharing your story. You are a survivor setting the world on fire with your truth. And, you never know who needs your light, your warmth, and raging courage."
~ Alex Elle

I got involved in the drug game at the early age of 7 or 8. Some might wonder how that is even possible. I used to hold large amounts of money for two or three drug dealers at the same time. How did this work? Well, I stood across the street from the drug dealers with a basketball or sometimes a football in my hand as they sold drugs to the users. When their pockets would start getting full, they would come across the street to me and pile their monies into my pockets. Why would they do this? They knew that at any moment the police could ride up, jump out and run through their pockets and either take their money or arrest them for selling dope. So they decided to place me across the street with the money because they knew that the cops would not even think that the little boy across the street playing with a ball had 12 to 15 thousand dollars inside of his pockets.

Each pocket sort of belonged to one of the drug dealers. Some might want to know; what was my pay for this foolish ordeal. My pay went straight to my mom, as the drug dealers would give her dope as my pay check. Just holding that money inside of my pockets felt so good that I had to have that feeling again. I fell in love with having lots of money and later in life this is one of the reasons I went to jail.

"Some habits you have come from things that have happened to you in your past, maybe as young as your early youth stages. Find the source of your habit and problem, and then you can combat it and you will overcome and conquer it."
~ *Marlo Da Motivator*

Being involved in drug dealing wasn't the worse shit that I experienced at such an early age. In fact, one of the worst things that I experienced around those years was being sexually abused by an older female family member. Let me go on the record and say that I do not hold this abuse against her and that I love her very much. I think that what she did to me, was something that someone did to her and I would be willing to bet that it may have been a family member that abused her. This sexual abuse that I went through was something that went on several times over the course of at least two or three years. This horrible experience is what I believed to have later in life help lead me to be so promiscuous. It even left a mental disconnect upon me as I grew older and as it relates to truly liking a girl for who she was. I did not really like girls for who they were. On the contrary, it lead me to only look for the sexual side of relationships. As I recount the sexual abuse, I can remember this person having me lick her vagina as she sucked my penis sometime in the sixty-nine style. Something that I learned from that is that when females have even a little hair in their vaginal area, as they pee it could get on the hair and leave a certain smell. That smell is something that I smelled on her and as I grew up I couldn't go down on a woman especially if I smelled anything that even remotely smelled like that. In fact, that whole experience made it hard for me to truly feel any true affection for females while I was having sex.

I never talked to my mother, dad nor sisters about the sexual abuse that I went through, but I made up inside of my mind that my children would never go through any shit like that. This is why I really didn't and still don't let my children spend a night at anyone's house except for my mother. For years I put this horrible sexual abuse that I experienced behind me, but one day my mother and I were talking and she told me something that blew my mind. She told me that she was raped as a teenager. I looked at her and I felt so sorry for her and with rage wanted to know if I could find that mutha fucka and kill him. Then she took it a step further and told me that one of my sisters is also my cousin. *Yeah you read that shit correctly.* She said that my uncle was the person that raped her and that she was too scared to tell anyone about it. In fact, she kept it a secret until the day that she went into labor with my sister as she sat on the toilet. The question that went through my mind is how could my own uncle do some stuff like this and from that day on I really didn't like that guy. However, as I sit here and write this as a grown man; I cannot help but wonder what it was that he had experienced inside of his life. Was he sexually abused? Was the abuse that he may have experienced afflicted on him by a family member? Ultimately, I decided to forgive him!

At some point I stopped holding the drug money for some of the dealers, in fact a few of them were killed. By 1988, we had lived in Oakland for three short years and we had moved or should I say had been evicted from 5 different apartments or houses all over Da Bottoms. My mom's drug habit caused her not to pay the utility bills and at times she didn't even pay the damn rent. One of the first times that I can remember our water being turned off was when we lived in West Oakland at 1560 5th street. The water company (EBMUD) shut our water off. My mom went outside, took the lid that covers the water meter in the ground at the curb off then turned the water back on. We had running water again. However, after a few days went past EBMUD realized that our water was back on, so they came back out and turned the water back off but this time they placed a lock on the meter. My mother not to be out done by them, or should I say to steal free water, went back outside and cut the damn lock right off of the meter and turned it back on again. Once again, we were able to take showers, drink water and wash the dirty ass dishes that had piled up. It was so bad that we had gnats flying all over the place. Well needless to say, EBMUD realized that we were using the water again without my mom paying the bill, so they came back out and they weren't fucking around this time. They went into the ground and removed the whole mutha fuckin meter. Have you ever looked in the ground where the water meter is supposed to be and only to see an empty hole? That shit was crazy mane! At that point I think that she just asked my dad for the money to get the water turned on.

After being evicted from the house on 5th street we moved several other times and finally ended up moving into the Salvation Army. By this time one of my sisters had had enough of this being evicted shit and the fact that my mom was spending the welfare monies on drugs before the damn check even came. So, she cut and moved in with one of her friends. Since we went in as a family of three, they allowed us to sleep in a small ass room with a bed in there. I think the people that came in as single had to sleep in a big ass room with hella people that they didn't even know. The Salvation Army was full of a lot of people and we had to share the bathroom with them. When it was time to eat, we had to go into the dining hall to eat at the tables with all of these people and I remember telling myself, "My kids will never have to do this shit!"

Let's Talk
"Learning About Ur Damn Self"

Many people have ideas as to what defines them whether it be a lot of money, a big house, a big booty, flat abs, a nice job or even something as simple as long hair. Take the time out to think about what it is that defines you.

What defines you?

_____
_____
_____
_____
_____

Life has and will continue to toss all kinds of wild tricks and curve balls at each and every one of us in this world and many people tend to swing at the balls and miss. Once they have swung and missed a few times they believe that they have struck out and that it is all over. They fail to realize that this is not a game. We're not playing baseball, this is real life. But if we were playing baseball, I will tell you that you will miss at times, but you got to get back in the batter's box.

How do you feel about the hard times that you have encountered?

_____
_____
_____
_____

Do you think you have struck out forever? If yes, why? If no, why not?

Do you think that you have been defined by those times? If so, how? If not, why not?

Many people in society look at famous and rich people as role models yet many of them have come from some of the harshest circumstances that we can think of and have faced things like homelessness, sexual and or physical abuse, addiction and yet they have made it to where they are today.

Despite of the harsh circumstances you have faced, what are you going to do to get to where you want to be?

_____

_____

_____

It is said that everyone has one, two or maybe even three people inside of their family that it is safe to say that they are off the hook. Some families have even more than three people that would come to the family function and simply mess everything up.

Did you grow up inside of a dysfunctional family? If so, list some of the things you would consider to be dysfunctional about it? If not, how do you think your family managed to stay functional?

_____

_____

_____

_____

_____

_____

_____

_____

_____

_____

_____

Please list three or four things that you have been through and or have witnessed within your family that may have shaped who you are today. This may or may not be something that many other people can say that they have experienced. Most people experience the same things, but in different ways.

From Da Bottoms 2 Da Top

1. _____

2. _____

3. _____

4. _____

Chapter 4
Your Setback Was You Being Setup For Your Comeback!

"Recycle your pain, allow your pain to reach you to greatness."
~Eric Thomas

f I had to tell anyone the worse time frame of my life, I would quickly state the year 2003 through 2004. Though I would say that this was the worst time frame of my life, I would be remiss if I didn't state that the things that I went through happened to make me a strong, great man with not only deep morals, but also a man of integrity and of great mental fortitude. I remember my mother going in and out of the hospital during this time on several occasions as she fought cancer after it had been in remission for the second or third time. On one occasion after receiving her chemo therapy, I drove her home. We sat in her room on her bed and as she was putting her fingers through her hair it started to come out. I remember her saying that this was embarrassing and I told her that I loved her so much as I collected her hair and placed it into a zip lock bag. She asked me why I was doing that, I didn't tell her why, but I knew that she wasn't going to be around for many more years. I still have her hair in a zip lock bag to this very day.

The few times that I was convicted of a crime was between 2003 and 2004, in fact I was arrested 4 times between 2003 and 2004. In 2003, I started to ask God to help me make a few vital decisions and for some strange reason I thought that one day I would wake up and God would have instantly removed the situation out of my life. Let me be the first to tell you that when you ask God for things, at times be prepared to go through some real growing pains. After the second time that I was arrested I told myself that this wasn't truly who I was and that I had to make some changes with my life. I remember sitting in Santa Rita County Jail and receiving a letter from my mother. She tried to catch me up on all of the things that were happening on the streets, but as she got to the end of her letter she said some words to me that pierced through to my soul. She said, "Son I know that you are better than this and I ask you, will the real Marlo please stand up?" I knew at that moment that I was not only letting my mother down, but also my two small daughters and myself.

Once I got out of jail, I stopped selling drugs, got rid of all of the illegal guns and got myself a job. I was still praying to God every day to help me make a decision as to which woman I should settle down with. I began to have headaches every day and had to take a pain pill daily just to make it through. My mother had most of our close family attending church and one day I went up to the pastor and asked him how he was able to be committed to one woman without cheating. He told me that not only does he love his wife, but moreover God called us to be faithful to one woman. That was easier said than done for me, however; I kept praying to God for help in that area. In early April of 2004 my mother decided to throw a get together for Easter and my sister's birthday. She was doing a lot of cooking and while she and I were in the kitchen, she started to cry and said that she did not want to die. She had a procedure that was coming up in the next two weeks which was supposed to not only help fight the cancer but it was going to help her hold down food on her stomach. She had not been able to hold down food for the last two weeks and they thought that it was a blockage that they would have to remove. She went to get the procedure and stayed in the hospital for weeks.

Three weeks later on May 1 2004, at around 1:15 a.m. I received one of the saddest phone calls that one could receive. My mother's doctor told me that there wasn't anything else that the hospital could do for her and that we have to let nature take its course. I asked him was she still alive and he said yes. I jumped up grabbed my youngest daughter and drove to the hospital expeditiously. She stayed alive for the next 5 and half hours which gave the family time to make it up there as she told all of us to work on our bad habits and to chase God with all of our hearts, mind and soul. She than passed away.

Truly, truly, I say to you, except a corn of wheat fall into the ground and die, it stays alone: but if it die, it brings forth much fruit.
John 12:24

We had my mother's funeral a week later which was May 8 2004, and as life would have it, the next day, we were all back at the same church to celebrate Mother's Day.

This was a very hard and sad time for us all. Ever since my mother had stop smoking drugs, cigarettes and drinking was the true backbone of the family. She had been clean for well over ten years and made a commitment to God to plant the seed about his goodness to all. That commitment was one that I personally watched her keep on a daily basis. She babysat everybody's kids, she drove everyone around, she came to help and recuse every one of us in the family when we fell on hard times. She became employed by the Oakland Unified School District, she bought a house, and she won Mother of the Year from the City of Oakland: she feed the homeless in the park, made sure that we all went to church, hosted every family gathering and was the one who was praying nonstop for all of her babies to win. Now she was gone! I believe God allowed my mother's death to push not only me but others in the family to step up and grow up, because she was always rescuing us out of shit.

My headaches became worse as I tried to take on her roll and keep the family afloat. One day my pastor called me and said that he had been praying and talking to God about how to get more men to come to church, namely bible study. God told him to have me lead it, which he said made good sense because he noticed how many men looked to me for advice and leadership. He went on to ask me if I would I do it. I told him yes, I would and I also asked him if he could teach me how to write sermons. I am not sure why I wanted to learn how to write sermons, but he said that he would teach me. He told me that the bible study supplies would arrive within a week and I could start teaching. Well, I was back in jail again before the week was out.

The day that I was arrested the damn headaches stopped. I still don't understand how and why this happened. How-ever, this time my short stance was over, I was sentenced to six years in prison. After sitting in the Santa Rita County Jail for 14 months I was awakened around 4 a.m. and told that I was being transferred to San Quentin State Prison. It had to be around forty inmates lined up at the back of the prison as correctional officers handcuffed and placed shackles on our legs. The handcuffs had a chain dropping from the middle of them as the chain connected to the shackles around our ankles. While on the bus (The Gray Goose) as it is called, the officers made it very clear that everyone on the damn bus better shut the fuck up. If not, they were going to pull the fucking bus over to make sure that the talkative person got the picture. There was one officer at the back of the bus inside of a gate with a long ass gun. There was the officer that was driving the bus who had a gun and another officer standing next to him with a gun in hand. The bus had a gate that was locked to separate the officers from the inmates. I must say that this was the quietest bus ride I ever took. I arrived at San Quentin State Prison and as soon as I seen this raggedy ass piece of shit looking compound, I was flabbergasted. This place seemed to look like if an earthquake was to happen that it would fall right over into the bay. I wasn't there for one month before a big ass race riot jumped off and a lot of people got hurt. I really don't know why the riot happened but from what I understand, someone didn't pay a debt for some damn tobacco. I just so happened to be headed for chow when it kicked off, and so I found myself caught up in this buffoonery. I also found myself in the hole for the next two weeks and then one early ass morning the correctional officer called my name and told me to pack it up. I was being transferred to High Desert State Prison all the way up north next to Reno in a city called Susanville.

I stayed in High Desert for about two months without seeing my family. Hell! I think that I spoke to my fiancé on the phone two or three times for about 8 mins or so the whole time while I was there. About three weeks before they transferred me to the next prison, I was told by a correctional officer to report to the counselor's office. As I walked into the office the counselor told me to have a seat and that he had some bad news for me. My mind started to race; what kind of bad news would this dude be about to tell me. Shit, my mother was already dead, I was sitting in a prison almost 6 hours away from my family and I still had about two more years to spend in prison. What the fuck do you got to tell me that's worse then what I am going through already? He told me that one of my sister's had died. Just as he said that, I sat down in disbelief and his phone started to ring. He answered it and handed me the phone. One of my other sister's started telling me what happened to my sister who died. Pain on top of pain.

"Prison Is Not An Option, Yet It Is Still A Choice!"
~ Marlo Da Motivator

I was finally transferred to California State Prison, Sierra Conservation Center, which is located in Jamestown CA. From the first day that I walked into that place I knew in my heart that I wasn't returning to jail or prison. In fact, I made up in my mind that I wasn't returning back into a prison or jail unless I was walking in on my own accord to visit someone and or to encourage someone about getting out and staying out. I began to read several books and I can remember in every single book that I read there was a famous quote inside of it. The quotes had much meaning to them and I found that each quote that I read was motivating to me. So much so that it pushed me and it wasn't long before I got enrolled inside of a carpentry training class in the prison because I knew that I had to pick up some sort of skill before returning home. I knew that there were not going to be a lot of open hands nor many well-paying jobs for a person coming out of prison. I got really good at carpentry so I asked to be transferred over to welding. I went into welding and learned how to do a few different types of welds, after that I asked to be transferred into a different training program. This time I transferred into auto mechanics as I figured that once I was released, I should be able to get a job building or tearing down real estate, if not I should be able to find some work wielding. I knew that the housing market was doing well and that someone would be able to use my skillset. However, I wasn't complacent and so I thought that it would be a great idea to also learn how to change brakes, tune-up a car and change car oil. I was getting an education and work ethic at the same time. The work ethic that I picked up helped me transition back into society without missing a beat. In fact, on my employment applications I even put down that I was attending school at Sierra Conservation Center which is a prison but the name itself happens to sound like a place that you might want to send your high school graduate to pick up some skills, a trade, a Career & Technical Education (CTE). I remember the manager at one company that I applied to read the skills that I picked up from Sierra Conservation Center's CTE program and was blown away. So much so that he said that he might try to talk his son into signing up to take some classes at the place. In my mind I was saying to this poor guy, no you don't want to send your kids there buddy. The fact that I put that info down actually made up for some of the gaps on my applications.

There was something great that happened in my life while being incarcerated at Sierra Conservation Center. My fiancée and I got married! We tied the knot right there inside of the visiting room and in this year 2020, we will be celebrating 14 years of a blessed and happy union. You know, I have heard many people say "don't marry a man that's in prison!" They say that incarcerated men simply use "prison talk" and will change up on the woman that stood by their side, once they are released from prison.

If I were asked to advise someone that was contemplating rather or not to marry someone that is incarcerated, I would tell them "not to put everyone in the same box!" Just because one person got out of jail and did the wrong thing, doesn't mean that everyone will do the same. Be careful, thoughtful, and prayerful while making that decision!

Wedding Day at Sierra Conservation Center
September 14, 2006

*35 Days Before My Release Date of
December 27, 2007*

Chapter 5
Admit Your Faults And Mistakes And Take Full Reasonability.

"Failure is a great teacher, and I think when you make mistakes and you recover from them and you treat them as valuable learning experiences, then you've got something to share."
~Steve Harvey

"'m steady tryna find a motive, Why I do what I do?, Freedom ain't gettin' no closer, No matter how far I go, My car is stolen, no registration, Cops patrollin', and now they done stop me, and I get locked up, They won't let me out, they won't let me out, (I'm locked up)." One day I was listening to the song by Akon called Locked Up and I had heard that song so many times over the years yet I missed the hidden message hiding in plain sight. The first eleven words that he said was very powerful. It was powerful enough for me to stop blaming my mother for smoking drugs which led to so many tough times that my sisters and I faced growing up.

I stopped blaming my dad for being a violent alcoholic that caused a lot of mental stress on me and didn't take out the time to come to any of my basketball games. I stopped blaming the teachers and school staff that didn't realize that I was a young boy that came to school tired and hungry due to my harsh living situations; that also didn't show me the love a kid in my situation needed. I stopped blaming the white man for all of the fucked up uneducated decisions that I made. Right there in that prison I took full responsibility for my errors and told myself that I must bounce back and be the real person that was on the inside of me the whole time. I simply had to put away the fake ass, pseudo mutha fucka I allowed myself to become.

- Nugget #1 - Acknowledge the hurt, pain and misfortune that you have encountered

- Nugget #2 - Forgive the offenders

- Nugget #3 - Accept your faults, mistakes and offenses

- Nugget #4 - Stop the blame game

- Then ask yourself two questions: Who are you and Why are you here??

I took time out to read as many positive books as I could every single day. I also made sure that I went to vocational/training classes every day even when I was sick and especially when I didn't feel like going. I wanted to make sure that I transformed my mental state to that of a hard working citizen, right there in that prison as much as possible. Don't get me wrong; I played basketball, I played chess, I played pinochle and conversed with people, but I made damn sure that I didn't do those things more than I worked on myself.

- Nugget #5 - Throw in the towel on the old person that you once proclaimed
- Nugget #6 - Step up and be the new and real you

Chapter 6
Who R U And Y R U Here?

"Don't be confused between what people say you are and who you know you are."
~ *Oprah Winfrey*

I can recollect being in the house one night with my mother, sisters and nephews; it was a night like any other when all of a sudden one of my sisters rushed into the front door screaming at the top of her lungs for my mother. Everyone in the house jumped up and ran towards the door to see what was going on. My sister told my mother to make all of us get back from the door and to go into the room because she didn't want for us to see what was on the other side of the door. My mom told everyone to get back and go into the room. Me being the hard head little guy that I was, wasn't about to not see what the hell was going on. So, I acted like I was going into the room, but I didn't go. What I saw was one hell of a scary sight. I recall my mother stepping out the door and letting out a scream and asking someone who did this to you. She stepped back into the house backwards with her arms outwards helping someone into the house. I quickly noticed that that someone was my cousin who my mother took in under our roof and raised as my sister for years. She was very bloody, her clothes were ripped into shreds as if they were put through a shredder. Her face and arms were all scrapped up and if memory serves me correctly, one of her shoes were missing.

They took her into the room, laid her down and my mother questioned her as to what happened. I do not remember if they even called the police or even took her to the hospital but I do recall learning what took place. This man that she had been dating for some time had turned himself into some sort of self-proclaimed pimp that was using some gorilla style pimping on her. According to her, she didn't want to go out and hoe up for him and he tried to force her to. She attempted to jump out of the car and he drove off with her hanging out of the door. She was dragged for a distance before getting free. What's even sadder is the fact that this wasn't the first time that he had treated her this way nor put hands on her, in fact he beat her on several occasions yet she decided to stay with him. I asked myself why she would stay with this abusive person and subject herself to all of this unjust pain. Yet as time went on, I remember my dad hitting my mother over the head with a tire iron and in the face with full beer cans. I hated my dad for doing those things and again I asked myself why would someone stay with this type of person?

As I grew older, I began to understand the answer to those questions and I also began to understand how difficult it is for many people to leave not only an abusive relationship but also any type of relationship that is not truly one that will make them a better person. I realized that not everyone has the mental fortitude to do so and many others are being held back by fear. I want to tell you to do what a book that I recall my wife once reading suggested. Feel the fear and do it anyway (Susan Jeffers 1987). I know that it is very hard to walk away. I even made the horrible and foolish error of slapping a woman before due to hurt and anger. I did the same damn stupid thing that I hated my daddy for doing to my mother. I want to state for the record that I was truly wrong and being hurt and angry does not give anyone and I do mean anyone the right to put hands on someone else. I was blessed enough to have also had the opportunity later on to speak to that individual and I was very grateful that she forgave me.

I must state that the question still remains today. Why would you stay with someone that hits you? I suggest that you ask yourself another question. Ask yourself; "who am I?" Then ask yourself, "why am I here?" I am willing to bet that you are a beautiful/handsome person. You are very intelligent, wise, strong, resilient, and powerful capable person. I know that you have had people in your life whether it be your mother, father, siblings, teachers, so called friends, co-workers or even your lover tell you that you were the opposite of these positive attributes, but you have to put their lie (that's right their lie, their untruth) to the side and focus on your truth. Write down all of the negative words that they have said about you and then I want for you to look up the antonym or the opposite word for each of the bad words. I want you to recite those new words (the antonyms) three times a day. Morning, noon and night. I also want for you to place them in areas around your house, cell, dorm, bathroom, etc. Put them in places that make it easy for you to see these powerful words about you. This is going to help you see and realize who you are.

> *"Who R U and Y R U Here?"*
> ~ *Marlo Da Motivator*

Once you have discovered who you are, you then have to figure out why are you here. Here can be in a bad unfruitful relationship, it could be a dead-end job, a prison or jail or maybe even being homeless. No matter what (your here is), you need to know why it is that you are there. The moment that you are honest with yourself about why it is that you are there I am more than sure that if you do the opposite of whatever it was that got you there, you will get out of there. Lastly, it is imperative that you are also willing to seek wise guidance and help from people and groups. I can assure you that there is a group, program or individuals that are waiting to help you get to the next level, but we often don't want to accept the life jacket due to the lack of trust, pride, or not wanting folks in our business, etc.

Look at it this way. If you are on a boat or ship sailing at sea and some-how you fall from the vessel and find yourself fighting for your life in the water. Then at some point you look up and see another vessel nearby, what would you do? I'm sure that you would try to get their attention. Once you have gotten their attention and they came near and tossed a life jacket out to you or held a long stick out to you for you to grab a hold of, would you grab hold of it? Again, I'm sure that you would reach out and grab hold of it so that you can be rescued. Well in the same way, you are drowning in this fucked up place/state that you find yourself in and often times there is help nearby, but you are not willing to reach out. I am telling you, I am asking you, I am begging you to reach out and take hold of your help line so that you can be you and be where you're supposed to be in life. I offer you an answer to the question that I asked you earlier, "Who are you?" You are a winner, you are a boss, you are not a failure; you are intelligent, beautiful, handsome individual on the way to your correct position in life.

Chapter 7
U Got 2 Have A Fuckin' Fight Plan!

"Tomorrow belongs to the people who prepare for it today."
~Malcolm X.

I remember doing some research on Sugar Ray Leonard and Marvelous Marvin Hagler. I wanted to know what led up to the big fight between the two men and how it was that Sugar Ray was able to beat him and recapture the championship belt after only having one fight in a little over 5 years. How was it possible for a man to have won 12 straight defenses of the belt, hold the highest knockout percentage of any and all acknowledged middleweight titleholders, at 78% yet lose a fight to a fighter who only had one fight in 5 years? You see Sugar Ray at the age of 25 years old found himself looking at a career ending medical situation. Ray was told that he had a detached retina and if he continued to fight, he could risk losing his eyesight. So, Ray did what many of us would have done; he walked away from the thing that he loved and did not fight again for over two years. While he was away Marvin Hagler started to gain even more notoriety, in fact he was kicking people's asses. Hagler was known as a hard puncher that had broken someone's jaw in the ring so not many people were lining up to fight him.

However, after being away from the game for two years Ray, decided to come back and take on a fight against Kevin Howard. This was a fight that Ray felt that he should have won with ease. However, during that fight Ray was knocked down even though he was able to finish the fighter off in the 9th round. However, afterwards he went ahead and retired once again. He stated that he did not have it any more, he just didn't have that same go get it, in him any longer. On the other hand, Hagler went on to take care of business and take care of business often. He won several fights during the five years that Ray wasn't fighting.

- What is it that you want to do and know that it is your calling to do, but you are not in the game?

- Who is doing the thing(s) that you should be doing and winning at it?

- How is it that they are able to go at it but you are not?

See these are some of the questions that you must ask yourself as you continue to read this chapter. In fact, I want you to write down the answers to these questions and save them as your phone background/wall paper, as the screen saver and wall paper on your laptop. I want you to see this shit all of the time. Understand this, while you are out of the game mutha fuckas are getting' it in and after you have read this book, and it motivates your ass to finally jump into the fucking game, you are going to have to compete at the highest level to take your rightful spot.

> *"For I know the plans I have for you," declares the Lord, "plans to prosper you and not to harm you, plans to give you hope and a future."*
> *~Jeremiah 29:11*

Ray came to the realization that he should be the champion and knew that he had what it took to not only compete at the highest level of boxing, but to also beat his competition. So, Ray decided to come back out of retirement to fight Hagler. In the course of the pre-fight negotiations Ray agreed to allow Hagler the larger share of the purse, in return Hagler granted Ray several conditions which turned out to be crucial to Ray's strategy to winning the fight. Did you just read what the fuck I just said to you? Focusing on the money Hagler unknowingly gave Ray the damn belt.

- What's more important to you? The money or your Dreams?
- I will submit to you, if you go after your dreams, the fuckin money will come.

What did Ray want in place of more money for the fight? Ray asked for a 22x22ft ring instead of the common 16x20ft size ring and to change the normal 15 rounds per fight down to 12 rounds for this fight. Ray also asked for other things that went on to help him in this fight, but I want to focus on the ring size in this chapter. Leading up to the fight, Ray knew that for him to beat Hagler he would have to come up with one hell of a fight plan. So, he decided to do the shit that the next man wasn't going to be willing to do. Ray starting bringing in sparring partners from everywhere and instead of sparring for 12 rounds he sparred for 15, sometimes 16 rounds. In professional boxing each round is 3 minutes in length, Ray declared that he would spar for 5 or 6 minutes each round. Ray even did some shit that mutha fuckas just weren't doing; he would box one partner for 3 or so rounds and then bring into the ring a fresh sparring partner to go for the next 3 or 4 rounds. He repeated this process throughout his training. These are fresh bodies and he was of course tired as hell, but he was building endurance and confidence. I am not sure what type of training Hagler was putting in, but I am willing to bet that it wasn't the same type of shit that Ray was doing. Keep in mind, Hagler had been whooping people's asses the whole time Ray was away and I am also willing to bet that Hagler didn't prepare as hard as he possibly could have, because he was the champ. Listen to me! "Don't let your winning streak blind your memory to all of the hard work that you put in to make it to your dreams."

- Are you that person that has worked hard your whole life or at some point in your life to reach a fuckin goal to only have reached it and now you are cruising?

- Have you lost your fuckin drive?

- Have you forgotten about how hard you busted your ass to get there?

About a week or so leading up to the fight Ray was sparring with one of his sparring partners and working on his fight plan. His fight plan was to go into the ring and prove that he could fight Hagler man to man in the middle of the ring. However, his sparring partner caught him with a good punch and put his ass on the canvas. Ray said that he damn near knocked him out. He said that all of his staff were very quiet and he knew what they were thinking. They were thinking that if his sparring partner can knock him to his ass, image what the champ is going to do to him. Ray said that he knew something that none of his staff knew, and that was that he was going to win the fuckin fight. At that moment

Ray realized something that we too must realize and that is that sometimes you will have to adjust your got damn fight plan. Ray decided instead of standing in the middle of the ring to fight Hagler and risk getting knocked out, he told his corner to do two simple things. He told them that he would pretty much dance around the ring for the first 2 and a half minutes of each round throwing a minimum amount of punches and he wanted them to yell out dip and slide (duck and slide over), every so often. He also told them to yell out 30 at the last 30 seconds of each round as he was going to pour out so many punches at Hagler's ass. With the larger ring which gave him more area to run around in and the plan to dip and slide and then pour out round ending punches Ray stole the fight.

- I am telling you that you must have a fight plan and you must be willing to adjust it at times so that you can reach your goal. Even more, you are going to have to be able to dip and slide as there will most definitely be people and circumstances that will come at you.

- You must also be willing to put in the work that the next mutha fucka isn't willing to do to get to your goal.

- Don't chase the money!

- Chase your dreams instead!

Chapter 8
(P.c.p) Persistence, Commitment & Perseverance

"Making your mark on the world is hard. If it were easy, everybody would do it. But it's not. It takes patience, it takes commitment, and it comes with plenty of failure along the way. The real test is not whether you avoid this failure, because you won't. It's whether you let it harden or shame you into inaction, or whether you learn from it; whether you choose to persevere."
~ President Barack Obama

I have watched and studied hella people over the years and spoke to many more and what I've learned is somewhat astonishing. People are not willing to bust their ass to win, but they are willing to bust their ass to get home to watch "Empire" or "How to Get Away with Murder." These same people love watching the "Have Nots" and "Sports Center."

They go to work every day for those long ass hours as they bust their asses to make the company richer, but won't put forth any real effort to chase their own dreams. I was once one of them mutha fuckas! One day all of that changed and my eyes were opened. I am not saying that I stopped working long and hard hours for the company, but I made the conscious decision to start working on myself and my dreams more and much harder than I would work on anyone else's dream and so should you.

When I got out of prison my fight plan was to do whatever it fucking took to do the right thing and take care of my family. My plan was not to return to prison unless I walked back in on my own accord to encourage others on getting out and staying out and then walking back out when I was ready to. This was not an easy task. Shit! I paroled right back to Oakland, right back in the damn hood and I could have easily jumped back into the game. I will submit to you that you have to be committed to what the hell you said that you were going to do and not going to do. I started working on starting my own landscaping business and as I was trying to put that together, money was short and bills were coming in. My wife was trying to hold it down and I wasn't going to just be a sucker and ask someone for help. Well, shit isn't that what we seem to call the mutha fucka in the hood especially a man who ask for help. There are a couple of other words that are used in the hood for that person as well. When I was on the street prior to the time I spent in prison I was the one that everyone came to asking for help and to ask for favors, but now I found myself in that situation. I humbled myself and called a friend that owned his own carpentry business and asked him for a job. He said I got you Marlo. When you went to jail you learned a trade, you didn't just waste your time in there and I could use your help. I stayed persistent, I could have easily thrown in the towel and said, "Fuck this square shit." He hired me and payed me around $10.50 to $11.00 per hour. Listen to me, you got to know your worth! I knew that I was worth more than what he was able to pay me, so I did my job, but I also went down to the DMV and got myself the handbook for commercial drivers. I studied that book daily and learned the rules and went back down to DMV and passed the Class A commercial test. I received my Class A permit and from there I got my first truck driving job and my pay doubled up to $21.50 per hour after only 4 months out of prison.

You know I remember once telling a group of about 80 to 90 inmates at a prison about how I got my first two jobs and one cat told me that I was lucky. I looked him straight in his fuckin eyes with love and told his ass that he was wrong as shit. I told them all that luck is when a mutha fucka is sitting at home and the CEO of some large ass company knocks on your door and asks you to come run his business even though you don't know him nor did you apply for the damn job. But what I did was prepare myself before I even left the damn prison for both of those opportunities. I didn't sit around in the prison and simply fuck off my time like many others did, on the contrary; I took my ass to three different trade classes and learned all three. I came home and asked for help and since I had the skills I was hired. I went to DMV and got the handbook and learned the rules as it relates to commercial driving and I was given a chance at a job after I took my ass into the company at three in the morning to complete the application. Fuck luck, go get what you want.

> *You may encounter many defeats, but you must not be defeated. In fact, it may be necessary to encounter the defeats, so you can know who you are, what you can rise from, how you can still come out of it.*
> ~ Maya Angelou

I worked that job for three years and then I was threatened to be fired because of my criminal record, but only after I brought up the discrimination that I was experiencing at the company. I left there and went to a different company and my pay went up again. Staying at the new job for a few years and once again leaving to a different job where my pay went up again. Out of prison for less than five years I bought my wife and kids our first house. I once again switched jobs and my pay went up again and I was making over $100,000 dollars a year. I enrolled in community college and obtained 3 certificates of completions and 5 different associates' degrees. I kept busting my ass and my annual pay went up to over $150,000 per year. I also began volunteering at San Quentin, Sierra Conservation Center and Deuel Vocational Institution which are three prisons within the California Department of Corrections & Rehabilitation. My family and I lived in the first house for three years and then my wife and I decided to buy a different house in a much safer and quaint neighborhood. You got to make sure that you make a commitment to yourself about achieving your goals and then you are going to have to be PERSISTENT as you chase them because shit is going to get hard on your ass. However, you will make it through and then you are going to have to persevere in your calling. As you can see, I am persevering in my calling because you are reading a book written by me: An ex-felon, ex-homeless, ex-dope dealer and ex-thief that barely graduated from a continuation school with a 1.87 grade point average.

Let's Talk
"Hard Times Makes You Bigger & Stronger"

Sequoias are said to be one of the biggest trees in the world. These trees are so tough that they grow very old, in fact their age is part of the reason that they grow so big. These trees just keep growing and growing as they get older and so should we.

Looking back at your past, have you seen any growth in your way of thinking? If yes, how so: If not, why not?

_____
_____
_____
_____
_____
_____
_____
_____
_____
_____

Have you seen any growth in the way that you react towards situations? If yes, how? If no, why not?

_____
_____
_____
_____

Have you noticed any growth in your communication with others? If so, how? If not, why?

These massive sequoias are only re-produced by seeds which occasionally stay in the cone for 20 years. One of the mind-blowing things about sequoias is that forest fires assist in opening the cones which then grow from the burnt, bare soil. Think of that, these grown giant sequoia trees are pretty much fire resistant and they reproduce as they get burnt. I am sure that you have been through many trials, problems and situations and whether you know this or not, you are made stronger as you go through the fire just like the fuckin tress. You are strong and you are a winner!

What were/are some of the hardest time(s)/fire(s) in your life (past/present)?

After you made it out of that fire(s) were you a weaker or stronger individual? If yes, how so? If no, why not?

_____
_____
_____
_____
_____
_____

Chapter 9
What Were You Called To Do?

"If God gives you something you can do, why in God's name wouldn't you do it?"
~ Stephen King

Over the past 11 years I have been driving around in some type of garbage truck picking up trash, green waste, food waste, dead animals, in addition to picking up recyclables while driving a recycle truck. One day I was driving down the street in the company's recycle truck knocking out my route and I heard a voice speak to me very clearly. It was the voice of God saying to me that instead of picking up garbage and recyclables you should be reaching out to and grabbing those folks that people treat and look at as garbage; recycling their minds and transforming their whole person!

> *"I believe there's a calling for all of us. I know that every human being has value and purpose. The real work of our lives is to become aware. And awakened. To answer the call."*
> ~ Oprah Winfrey

Before God spoke to me in the truck I had been going to speak at prisons, parole departments, at risk adult and youth programs but not full time. I would take off of work to go out and speak or leave work early missing out on a full day's pay so that I could go and reach folks. However, after God told me that I should be truly grabbing those folks that some people look at as nothing more than trash, I went full speed towards it. You know many people claim to be saved and followers of Christ yet once they hear that a person is in jail, prison or have been previously incarcerated many people don't want to fool with that person. For some strange reason they forget about Matthew 25:36-40 in the bible when Jesus stated "I needed clothes and you clothed me, I was sick and you looked after me, I was in prison and you came to visit me." Then the righteous will answer him, 'Lord, when did we see you hungry and feed you, or thirsty and give you something to drink? When did we see you a stranger and invite you in, or needing clothes and clothe you? When did we see you sick or in prison and go to visit you? "The King will reply, Truly I tell you, whatever you did for one of the least of these brothers and sisters of mine, you did for me."

Some others also have forgotten that Moses could have been incarcerated if he lived in today's times. Yeah, "I said it!" He once killed a man and buried him in the sand. Last time I checked that would have him serving time in San Quentin State Prison. Many others have forgotten that David a person that God called a man after His own heart once sent a man to war, put him on the front line so that he could be killed so that he could get the man's wife. That sounds like 2nd or 3rd degree murder to me. He would have been sitting in High Desert State Prison or something. What about Peter? He walked with Jesus, but he also cut a man's ear off with a sword. Now I am not the smartest person in the world, but that is definitely mayhem. That shit would have had him sitting up in Corcoran State Prison. Let's not forget about Paul. You see Paul's name used to be Saul and before it was changed to Paul he used to stand there holding the coats in approval of the people that were killing Christians. Now that sounds like accessory to murder like a mutha fucka. He would have been sitting in Pelican Bay State Prison. My point is very simple. We must not turn our backs on people because they have made a mistake or an error. Many of strong leaders, entrepreneurs, great fathers and mothers, singers, actors, pastors, yeah, I said pastors, have made errors and have bounced back at some point in their lives. I just so happen to understand that and I am taking on that calling to not only come visit my people that are incarcerated, but to come lift you up and recycle your person so that you will be the best you.

Marlo Speaking to a group of Gentlemen doing time in Sierra Conservation Center (Prison in Jamestown CA)

I used to work and drive for this company out of San Francisco and it was my duty to pick up the old meat from stores like Costco, Safeway, Lucky's; even mom and pop meat markets. I would load all of that old stinky meat into the back of the truck which was shaped just like your local garbage truck and take it back to the plant. Make no mistake about it, it was a very stinky truck! It was so stinky that when I would drive down the street people in their cars and people walking down the street used to cover their noses. In fact, I remember sitting at a stop light one day and a police officer pulled up next to me in his patrol car and began looking over and up at me (I was sitting higher up because I was in a truck). He rolled his window down and motioned for me to roll my window down as well. I rolled down my window and he asked me how in the hell can you drive a truck that smell so fuckin bad. I looked him dead in his face and told him that all I smelled was money. I used to have birds flying down the street chasing the truck every day because they loved to eat the meat that got stuck to the sides and top of the truck.

Once I got the old meat or tallow (which is the common name of it) back to the plant, I would roll up a large door and back the truck up to a large pit to unload the tallow into the pit so the pit operators could begin the process of grinding up the material. The material would then slide down the machine to another machine and once this bloody stinking stuff made it to the other machine they would somehow turn it into a fine powder and ship it overseas to places like China. China would than use the tallow or should I say the fine powder to make things like pet food, soap, cooking oil, candles, lip stick, mascara, etc. Yep, I said it women mascara! We take some of the most stinky, bloody, nasty looking shit in the world and turn it into things that make us smell good, things to help us cook food, things that beautify us. In the same way we as people must remember that we are called to take those of our society that are looked at as trash, put them through a processor of rehabilitation, so they too can be used to beautify the world just like that old ass meat. Wouldn't you agree that a human restoring another human so that person could be reused for great things, is much more important than humans restoring and reusing old ass meat to make dog food or some fuckin mascara?

Chapter 10
Get Off Of The Fucking Treadmill

"Jogging in place on a treadmill may be good for your health, but that shit could prove to be a waste of your time if you aren't chasing your dreams on the damn pavement."
~ Marlo Da Motivator

    Many people say that they want to accomplish a lot of different things in life, yet the moment you ask them why they haven't reached their goals, they will tell you all type of bullshit and excuses. I once heard a wise man say that "Excuses are for mutha fuckas who expect to lose!" (T.I.). I know people that have stated that they were going to start a business, get a job, a GED or even a high school diploma to look up many years later and not have done shit. So, I have a couple of very simple questions for you. What have you been or what are you running towards? Are you making any ground? Do you see the end of the tunnel? If the answer is no, I want you to take out the time to look the fuck down:

you will never make any ground if you are running in place. I happen to believe that your ass is on a damn treadmill and it's time to get the fuck off. Your treadmill could be an unhealthy ass relationship, a horrible job or your treadmill could be lies. It could be those cheap ass lies that you have been telling yourself for months and or years. Come on, you know what I am talking about. Aren't you tired of saying that you just don't have enough time to go back to school or look for a different job? Why don't you put down the fuckin X-Box or Play Station controller, which would give you a little extra time to get something positive accomplished? Instead of looking at social media all damn day, why don't you take a look at a website that employers post job openings on? Don't just sit in the damn prison and play pinochle and chess all day. It's time to get busy and apply yourself by getting into the CTE (Career & Technical Education) program, and or the High School or GED programs.

I was arrested on September 9, 2004 and returned home on December 27, 2007 and I must tell you that most of the fuckin people that I knew were still in the same damn position in life that they were in when I left. In fact, some of them mutha fuckas were worse off than they were before I left. Why is that? Because they were running on that treadmill. I was able to within five months surpass most of the people that I knew. How was that possible? First of all, I will give all thanks to God for blessing me and people in my life that were willing to assist me and secondly I got busy. I worked my ass off, I went through some stressful times, but not once did I expect to lose. I am a got damn winner and so are you!

Do you expect to lose? Don't you even think about answering the question? I already know the answer to that shit. If you have made it to this part of the book then I know that you not only expect to win, but that you are not going to continue to stand on that fuckin treadmill. In the early part of this book I spoke about some lyrics from a song of Akon and I must tell you that we have to revisit them. "I'm steady tryna find a motive why I do what I do?" I happen to believe that it is of the utmost importance that you find the motive as to why you do what you do. Now after you have found the motive that leads you to do what it is that you are doing, then you need to find the motive that leads you to not do what you should be doing.

For example: if you are not taking care of your kids, what's stopping you? This is something you should be doing! You must also figure out why you continue to put yourself through foolish bullshit? I am willing to submit to you that you put yourself through bullshit because you feel that it is easier. Please understand this; you are not the only person that takes the easy way out. However, today all of the taking the easy way out of shit for you has stopped.

Let's Talk
"Are you ready?"

My mother smoked cigarettes my whole life. There were several times that she said that she was tired of smoking that shit and she would claim to be quitting. This shit happened so much that I simply stopped paying attention to her when she said that she was quitting. I remember one time that she decided to put on a Nicorette patch to help her stop smoking. That shit didn't work so she got herself some fuckin Nicorette chewing gum believing that it was the magic trick to cure her damn issue. Well, that shit didn't work either and the next thing that I know, her ass was wearing the Nicorette patch, chewing the Nicorette gum and smoking a cigarette at the same damn time.

Then one day she got the news that she had cancer. Do you know what she did? She stopped smoking. Why? What happened? I'll tell you what happened. She got to the point where she had to quit. She was pushed to be finally ready.

Have you made it to the point where you have to quit? If yes, explain? If no, why not?

_____
_____
_____
_____
_____

What negative habit(s) do you have that you have not admitted to yourself that you have or what habit(s) do you have that you have recently discovered were negative?

_____

_____

_____

_____

_____

_____

Are you ready and willing to overcome them?

_____

_____

_____

_____

_____

_____

If so, write down your fight plan on how you're going to overcome them? If not, write down what's holding you back and what it will take to help you develop a fight plan. Let's not forget that my mother waited until she had cancer to develop a fight plan.

_____

_____

_____

_____

_____

Chapter 11
Fuck Fear

"You have upon you the worst enemy that a man can have, and that enemy is fear."
~Malcolm X

I began playing basketball in the 5th grade, however; a lot of my childhood friends started playing the sport several years earlier. I remember we used to play pick-up basketball at the park or in the school playground and as the captains picked their teams, I was nervous as shit. It wasn't that I was nervous because I thought that I wouldn't get picked to be on a team, but I was nervous because I didn't want to mess up in the game. I didn't want to miss a shot, double dribble or travel. To me, if I committed one of those violations, I would be looked at as weak as hell. I had this same mentality when I started playing organized basketball. The fear inside of me got worse when my team got on the court for the pre-game warm-ups. I remember being so damn fearful that I used to shiver; it was bad. My fuckin teeth use to gnash together as we ran the layup line. Interesting enough, once I started to run up and down the court I would forget about the damn fear and try to do what I was supposed to do and that was play basketball. This same fear on the court actually fucked with me throughout my whole high school basketball career. I happen to believe that I would have been a much better player if I wasn't so damn scared. Why was I so scared? I wasn't scared to fight, sell drugs and or run around with guns, but when I got on that fuckin court, man was I scared. Why did I allow the fear of making a mistake drive me crazy even before taking the court? I think the reason that I allowed fear to get the best of me is the same reason why many people allow fear to stop them from going for their dreams. That is the fear of making a mistake or things not working out.

For example: when we were younger, my sisters and their friends use to jump rope and at times my friends and I would come over, and jump right in the ropes without hesitation. It was fun until they switched over to double-dutch, which at that point I would simply just quit. They would ask me to jump in, yet I would stand at the edge of the ropes rocking back and forth trying to find the correct time to jump the fuck in. I would do this back and forth motion for so fuckin long, that someone else would simply jump in right in front of my ass. This is the same shit that is happening to you in life right now. You are always trying to find the right time to get shit started or completed, and while you are hesitating someone else is jumping in right in front of you. Though you want to start that business, write that book, quit that job and or walk away from that miserable relationship; you stay still waiting on a good time to do it. I want to tell you to do the same shit my sister and friends did when we played double-dutch. Just jump the fuck in! Once you get going you will forget about the fear just like I did while playing basketball. Like I mentioned in one of the earlier chapters, my wife once read a book that said feel the fear and do it anyway (Susan Jeffers 1987). So, feel the fear and do it anyway!

Some of you may be thinking, Marlo that shit sounds good, but I am too damn old to be trying that now. Other folks might be saying, Marlo I tried over and over again and I just cannot seem to be able to grab that dream of mine. You might also be saying, Bruh! I have been called stupid all of my life; I did not graduate from school nor do I have a GED. Still some of you are yelling out what if what I am trying to accomplish doesn't work out and I lose money and time. Well I have a few questions for you. Have you ever heard of Colonel Sanders? It is recorded that his recipe was shot down time and time again, yet he kept pushing it. He didn't even become rich until he was well in his late 70's or early 80's. Now there are over 23,000 KFC's around the world. What if he gave the fuck up? My second question is, have you ever heard of WD39? I am sure that you haven't heard of WD39 because that shit doesn't exist, it's called WD40. Now I know that you have heard of WD40 and you may have also used it in the past to stop your door from squeaking or to remove rust from something. How do you think WD40 got its name? It is called WD40 because it took them 40 tries to get the formula correct. Which means that they messed up 39 times before finally getting it right. Just imagine if they would have given up and thrown in the towel on the 38th or 39th try. They would not be a multi-million-dollar company that's on the stock exchange market today. Now let's take a look at Thomas Edison's. It is said that his teachers told him that he was too stupid to learn anything. Does that sound familiar? Hell, the man was even terminated from the first few jobs that he had because they said that he wasn't getting shit done in a timely manner. Well Thomas Edison is known as the mutha fucka who happened to invent one of the first light bulbs. What people don't talk about is the fact that it took his ass 1,000 tries to successfully invent the damn light bulb. Yeah you read that correctly. He tried and failed at making the light bulb 999 times and on the 1000 attempt he got it right. He was once asked by a reporter how did it feel to fail 1000 times and he replied I didn't fail 1000 times. The light bulb was a process that had 1000 steps. Are you a few steps away from obtaining your ultimate goal? I don't give a shit if you have been arrested 40 times, you still have another opportunity to do things the right way. Do it! I don't care that you have had three divorces, maybe just maybe the right person for you is right in front of your face. So what if the last five businesses that you tried to start didn't take off, you have another idea inside of your head and it just might be the fuckin winner. FUCK FEAR……. GO AFTER YOUR DREAMS AND DON'T EVER GIVE UP!!!!

Chapter 12
Open Letter

It is my hope that this letter finds and reaches you in good health. I know that you are at a stage in your life where you are tired of being locked up and you want to truly live out the life that you were called to live. I want to take this time out to tell you about how things are going out here. This may or may not surprise you but most people are pretty much in the same spot and position that they were in the past. Not many people have truly went after their dreams and can tell you with all honesty that they consider themselves really successful. I once heard a wise man state that he defines success as doing the thing or things that you love to do and then finding someone to pay you to do it (Les Brown). Listen to me! Based simply on that definition, not many people are successful. My friend, what is success to you? Do you see yourself ever reaching that success? What would it take for you to reach it? What is stopping you from grabbing it right now?

I understand what it feels like to be locked up and told by others what time you have to go eat breakfast, lunch and dinner. I know what it is like to be told that you cannot use the phone right now because it is not phone time. I also know what it is like to not get visits. Understand this, I know what it is like to be looked at as a leper or even feeling like you are not part of main society. The feeling of not being in control of when you can and cannot take a vacation, is a feeling I know all too well. Being unable to go to your children activities without asking the boss is it okay, is truly deflating. However, please know that I not only believe that you will get out of that prison, but that you will also grab success and then help others do the same.

A few weeks before I got released from prison, I made a decision to write down on a piece of paper all of the shit that I hated about jail and prison. As I got closer and closer to my release date, I began to hate being there more and more each day. You will be surprised at how much shit you hate about something, especially when you are close to leaving. I would fill up a whole sheet of paper about the things that I hated about being incarcerated and then I would send the notes in the mail home to my wife, as I asked her not to open them. I told her that I wanted to open them for myself so I could remind myself of the shit that I made it through, and to remind myself to never go back. After being home for a few days from prison, my plan wasn't working out like I wanted it to, I was discouraged and thought about going out to get some quick money. However, one day I went to the door to check the mail and I received a letter written by Marlo while in prison to Marlo on the streets. This letter woke my game up! This letter kicked me into second gear! I got back on the grind and went out to ask for help and got my first job.

Then the LORD answered me and said: "Write the vision and make it plain on tablets, That he may run who reads it.
~Habakkuk 2:2

Do me and yourself a big favor. I want you to ask yourself a few questions and then answer them. Write it out so that you can see the answers. Trust me this here works!

- How long have I been locked up?
- How much more time do I have?
- What is my fight plan?
- What are some of my potential distractions?
- It's not if the distractions come, it's when they do come, how can I adjust my fight plan?

Now that you have started on the road to success, I need you to write down your release date. I think some of you may be somewhat confused as to who it is that I am writing this letter to. I even feel that some of you may simply skip this letter because you seem to think that I am not talking to you. Make no mistake about it, I am talking to you. Yep that's right, You! Let's be clear, you do not have to be locked behind prison bars or in a physical cell to be a prisoner. There are many people who are imprisoned while they are sitting right in the comfort of their fuckin living room. Some of you have been imprisoned for the last 20 years at the same dead-end job. There is another person that is imprisoned in that fucked up so called relationship. Oh yeah, let's not forget about the person that finds him or herself living the so-called dream life with a lot of money, friends and family but are not truly happy. They maybe be mentally broke and cannot seem to find their way out of that mental prison. You are the one that I am writing this letter to. You need to figure out your parole date. In fact, fuck parole, you have maxed out your sentence and will now be freed without parole.

Let's Talk
"How 2 Stay Da Fuck Out!"

When I got released from prison I realized that the only way that I was going to stay out was to follow my fight plan and to also stay away from old things and people. I knew that it was of the utmost importance for me to not go back to the same old relationships, so I stayed clear of them. In fact, even to this day, after all of these years, I still run into people that I haven't seen in a long time and they ask me: "Did you just get out of prison?" After talking to them a few minutes and doing a thorough inventory of them, meaning I pay full attention to their swagger and their so-called hustle. I look to see if they are on the up and up, if they are talking about positive things etc. If I see that they are out in the streets and they do not seem to want to change I take note.

Many of times they will say to me, "Marlo let me get your number and I will hit you later." If I discern from our conversation that they are still about that street life, what do you think that I give them? Well I'll tell you. I give them the wrong mutha fuckin number! I know that I do not need to be in any relationship where the person and or business is doing negative illegal shit and neither should you!!!

Who do you need to stay away from so that you can stay free? Don't get it twisted this person may even be in your family; your mother, father, brother or sister.

_____

_____

_____

_____

Make no mistake about it, some people cannot go around night clubs because they cannot control themselves, while others cannot go around liquor or drugs.

What do you need to stay away from so that you can stay free?

_____
_____
_____
_____
_____

Get involved in something that you can give back to. It doesn't matter if it is volunteer work because at some point you will realize that you have a responsibility to those who are depending on you and that responsibility can help you keep making the right decisions.

What can you involve yourself in that can give you a sense of extra responsibility and take up some of your time?

_____
_____
_____
_____
_____

Real Life Scenario #1

Person A arrives at one of their auntie's house to visit, but she is not at home. On the contrary, Person B someone that Person A haven't seen in a very long time is there, and the both of them began talking. Person B is a person that Person A had a very good relationship with, yet due to life and different circumstances, the both of them just didn't stay in touch. Person A noticed that Person B was still into illegal activities, selling weed without a license, and carrying illegal firearms.

They continue to converse with each other for a few minutes, because they were reminiscing and having a good time. While talking about all of the good times that they had in the past, the Person B cell phone rings. Once Person B gets off of the phone, he/she states that that was their kid on the phone and that they have to go pick him/her up from the train station and asks Person A to ride with him/her.

Keep in mind that not everyone has the courage to say no to people because they feel like they might hurt the others person feelings or they feel like they might sound like a square.

What advice would you give to Person A? Person A lacks the courage to say no: How can the person get out of this situation?

_____
_____
_____
_____
_____

Marlo Da Motivator

How I Got Out Of The Situation!

I said ok let's go get her. As we started to walk out of the house, I grabbed my cell phone out of my pocket, and switched it to silent mode. I then put the phone up to my ear and said hello. I stopped walking and lifted up my pointer finger singling for him to hold up. I was quite for a few seconds and then into the phone I asked: Where is he now? I waited for a few more seconds and then said: Can I speak to him please? The person that I was about to get into the car with in a low voice asked me: "Is everything okay?" I replied "not sure yet." I then began to act like I was talking on the phone again and said that I was on my way now. I put my phone into my pocket, and told the person that I was about to get into the car with, that I cannot go with him, because I have to go grab my son from school. I told him that my son had been in a fight, and I had to pick him up now.

We hugged and went our separate ways. Now I know that some people may be thinking that all of that wasn't necessary, and you may be correct. However, I want for you to know that it is better to get out of a situation that can lead you to jail or dead by making up an untruth than to take that chance.

Real Life Scenario #2

A parolee is standing outside of his/her home and a few of his/her friends that are still into illegal shit pull up, jump out and began to talk to him/her. The friends tell the parolee that they are about to go to the mall to pick up a few items and ask the parolee to come with them.

Once again, keep in mind that not everyone has the courage to say no to people because they feel like they might hurt the others person feelings or they feel like they might sound like a square.

What advice would you give the person that lack the courage to say no? How can the person get out of this situation without actually saying no?

_____
_____
_____
_____
_____

A Quick Way Out

Blame the parole agent! Yeah, I said it, blame the parole agent. Trust me, your parole agent want get a fuck if you blame him/her! Take a look at the time on your phone or watch and then tell them that you would go with them but you are waiting on your parole agent that is supposed to arrive at whatever time your phone displayed when you looked at it. Tell them that the parole agent is coming to conduct a site visit on your house and that the parole agent told you he/she was coming with 5 or 6 other agents, and they are going to search your house and anyone with you. Let them know that after the parole agents leave, you will roll with them if they want to chill and wait with you while the parole agents' searches everything. Watch how fast those mutha fuckas get away from you!

Chapter 13
Don't Waste Time And Don't Quit

Now that you are free, you have to chase after your dream(s) and one way that you can begin doing this is by going to bed 20 minutes earlier. If you go to bed 20 minutes earlier then you can set your alarm clock to wake you up 20 minutes earlier. Now if you are like most people, you will probably push the fuckin snooze button at least once every day so that you can get that extra 15 minutes of sleep. Whether you get up when your alarm initially goes off or get up after you take that 15 minute snooze, just get up and start writing that book, song, story or rap that you are supposed to write. You can work on that innovative idea or business that the world is waiting on you to put out. Listen to me, that extra 20 minutes a day adds up to 2 hours and 20 minutes a week. You will start seeing progress towards you dream and at some point you are going to stop pressing that fuckin snooze button because you will actually start to believe that you can accomplish your dream and that extra 15 minutes every morning that you were fuckin wasting on sleep will add up to be 1 hour and 45 minutes per week. Now let's do the math, 2 hours and 20 mins plus 1 hour and 45 mins a week adds up to 4 hours and 5 minutes a week of working on your dream while still going to work to survive. This might not sound like much but it is a hella of a lot closer to your dreams than you were at first.

Do not be deceived, this chasing your dream shit is not going to be easy. In fact, this shit is hard and at times I myself thought about giving up on this shit and to just go back to focusing on my job, you know my 9 to 5. Just keep collecting the weekly pay check from them. Collecting that check from work seemed so much easier, and it was what many call "Fasho' money." Yeah, we can call it fasho' money until the job decides to fire our ass or they go out of business. Then What?" As I write this I am reminded about a statement or quote that I once read somewhere. It said something along the lines that "You can bust your ass working hard towards making someone else's dreams come true and earn a living, or you can bust your ass working hard to make sure your dreams come true and earn a fortune!"

Which one do you choose? Since you are choosing yourself and your dreams remember, this shit is going to be hard, if it wasn't hard everybody else that you know would be doing it. You are going to have to talk to yourself when you feel like giving up. Tell yourself to push forward and listen to motivational speakers and others who have accomplished big shit. You are going to have to talk to people that believe in you, that will encourage you to keep going. You are going to have to cry, feel sad, get mad, and yet keep digging. Money will most likely run short, and so will some of your so-called friends, patience, food and sleep, but don't quit! You will make it to your goal. One of my goals was to have my own television show and, on that show, I was going to share my story and also have others come on the show to share their life stories. Well look, you are reading my book. It never crossed my mind to write a book and yet my story is still getting out all the same. I will get that television show one day, but on the way to it, other great things are happening and the same will happen for you.

Just remember:

"It's not where you start that defines you, you're defined by what you make of it."

I came from Da Bottoms, (The Lower Bottoms), 2 Da Top (Top of the World)! Come on up here, it's a helluva view!

www.ingramcontent.com/pod-product-compliance
Lightning Source LLC
Chambersburg PA
CBHW040527120526
44589CB00050B/2788